The *Unofficial* Dyson DC07
Workshop Manual

The *Unofficial* Dyson DC07 Workshop Manual

All you need to know to perform any DIY repair to your Dyson DC07

Angus Black

Scruton Publishing

Published by Scruton Publishing & Media. Hyde House, 193 Market St, Hyde, Cheshire, SK14 1HF, England.

First published 2011

ISBN 978-0-9556874-1-9

Printed and bound in Great Britain

DISCLAIMER

The author intends that this book be relied on purely as a helpful stepping stone on the path to education on the subject matter. Neither the author nor the publisher accept any legal responsibility for the adequacy, accuracy, completeness or reasonableness of any of the information, statements, opinions or comments referred to or contained within this book nor for any damage or loss, howsoever caused directly or indirectly occasioned by any such reliance. Nothing in this publication excludes or limits the publisher's liability for death or personal injury caused by its negligence, for fraud or fraudulent misrepresentation, or any other liability that cannot be excluded or limited under applicable laws.

The opinions expressed are the author's own and any examples contained within this book are for illustrative purposes only. All work to electrical appliances should only be carried out by competent, qualified people in accordance with their local laws. Faulty electrical appliances can cause serious personal injury and death. Always take the relevant precautions, and if in doubt, consult an experienced engineer.

Any website referred to in this work as a potential source of further information does not mean that the author or the publisher endorses the information the website may provide or recommendations it may make. Readers should be aware that any internet websites referenced may have changed or disappeared between when this work was written and when it is read.

The information contained in this book may differ from the opinion of Dyson Limited. Working on your Dyson vacuum cleaner as described in this book will probably invalidate any Dyson warranty you may have. Neither the author nor the publisher is connected to, or in any way affiliated with Dyson Limited.

Contents

Introduction... 1

Chapter One The Basics — Model Variants and Simple Maintenance 5

Chapter Two General Troubleshooting 14

Chapter Three The Brush Roll, Belt and Clutch............................... 29

Chapter Four The Cyclone Unit 49

Chapter Five Replacing the Motor 62

Chapter Six The Wand and Back Hose 81

Chapter Seven The Chassis and Sundries..................................... 90

Chapter Eight Where to Source Parts and Machines 95

Chapter Nine Other Resources and Further reading 103

Introduction

The Dyson DC07 was the fourth upright vacuum cleaner produced under the Dyson brand name. (There was a vacuum cleaner by James Dyson that pre-dated the DC01 called the G-Force, but it was licensed to a Japanese company called Apex Inc., and only available on the Japanese market.) The first upright Dyson branded machine was the DC01, the second was the DC03 and the third was the DC04. Dyson took everything they had learned with the DC01, DC03 and the DC04 and improved on it to make the DC07. (The DC02 was not an upright – it was a cylinder machine in case you wondered.)

The DC07 has the improved Root Cyclone system and washable pre-motor filter fitted as standard. Whilst the design is quite similar in many respects to the earlier DC04, they improved the cyclone design, the bin emptying mechanism and a few other minor design features.

Released in the earlier part of this millennium, the DC07 was given the slogan "the original Root Cyclone upright" because this was the first implementation of Root Cyclone technology into a vacuum cleaner. (Root Cyclone is called Radix Cyclone in Australia, most likely because "root" is a slang term for sex in Australia.)

Many people were confused as to whether this technology was any different from the previous Dual Cyclone technology from the DC01 and DC04. The cyclone itself – the clever bit – features seven narrow chambers inside the main unit. Earlier models did not feature this design. The multi-chamber design was a winner, an idea Dyson has stuck with, as they still use a similar design in their current models. The DC07 was available in a wide variety of colours, and still represents a great value reconditioned buy – or DIY project – today.

Dyson's Root Cyclone technology separates dirt from the air using centrifugal force. It doesn't rely on a filter or a paper bag to separate the dirt from the fast-moving air passing through it, so suction remains constant, even when the machine is nearly full.

The DC07 has a trigger operating a flap on the bottom of the bin to empty, it is easier to use with the tools, and the tools are stored on-board in a far more sensible way than with the earlier models. Most people find it is just a nicer machine to use than the earlier models, although some ladies – as with many upright Dysons – complain they are a little heavy to carry around the house and especially up the stairs.

Due to the fact that Dyson has traditionally had quite long product warranties and decent after sales service, they were able to control much of the after-market, both with parts supply and service work. They were presumably reluctant to release much in the way of service information, exploded drawings and the like, except to their own approved dealers.

Some after-market parts manufacturers have found themselves in legal hot water defending intellectual property claims for making parts Dyson didn't approve of. Dyson has not always won these cases, and slowly but surely, lower-priced alternatives to many original parts have come on to the market.

What was missing was a workshop manual as you can buy for most cars should you choose to do your own service and repair work. There was no book available that showed the practically inclined person how to perform the most popular repairs a Dyson is likely to need over its infinitely extendable lifetime. Whilst there are a few internet sites hosting incomplete (and often incorrect) information, nobody ever wrote the whole thing before. I have addressed that problem. You are holding it in your hands!

Dyson vacuum cleaners are respected across the world, not only as British designed products of which we British can be proud, but as innovative pieces of highly capable engineering in their own right. Certain limited edition models have even been described as art. Indeed, a mint condition purple, yellow and red DC01 or DC04 De Stijl model can command an increasing premium amongst those who appreciate neoplasticism and the abstract designs and bold colour combinations that are typical of that concept.

The good news for you — whichever model you own — is that your Dyson need never die. There is nothing that can go wrong with your machine which if you are practically inclined, and have a fundamental grasp of home electrics, you cannot source the parts and repair yourself for a fraction of the cost of a new Dyson. More importantly, armed with this book, you will have the information you need to get it right the first time and have your Dyson up and running again quickly — without breaking the bank.

The information in this book is primarily based upon UK market Dyson DC07 vacuum cleaners. Overseas models tend to differ very little for our purposes — often not at all — and so the information herein is equally valid for machines in any country.

In recent times, people are not only keen on saving a few pounds, dollars or euros by repairing things themselves, they are becoming increasingly aware of the damage we do to our environment by needless waste. It is claimed that each of us throws away over three tonnes of broken electrical appliances during the course of our lives. Repairing and extending the life of your Dyson is green. It's a small cog in the large machine that is our future sustainability.

For our American readers, I should make a note about the language in this book. The English in this book is primarily British English. Most of you will have no difficulty with that – but some words can differ. If American, treat the words "cable", "flex" and "lead" as interchangeable with "cord". A "mains lead" is what you know as a "power cord".

Where prices are mentioned, they are mostly in UK £ Sterling, sometimes referred to as GBP.

Chapter One
The Basics — Model Variants and Simple Maintenance

There are fifteen UK models of Dyson DC07, and a few other variants supplied to other countries around the world. This is not as confusing as it may seem at first glance. The variations mostly comprise which extra tools and accessories were supplied with the machines originally, which filters they were fitted with, the colour of the unit, and if the model is clutched (a brush control mechanism operated by a clutch allowing the brush roll to be switched off) or not.

Here is a list of the UK market models with colour variants:

- DC07 Standard. Grey/Yellow.
- DC07 Origin. Silver/Yellow.
- DC07 All Floors. Grey/Blue.
- DC07 Precision. Silver/Black.
- DC07i. Purple/Yellow or Silver/Red
- DC07 Allergy. Purple/Green, Purple/Red or Purple/Blue.
- DC07 Animal. Silver/Lavender.
- DC07 HEPA. Silver/White.
- DC07 Clic. Three Tone Pink.
- DC07 Tool Kit. Silver/Blue
- DC07 Full Gear. Silver/Red
- DC07 Full Kit. Purple/Lavender/Grey.

Most of you will be more than familiar with how your Dyson operates and how to use it. However, many people acquire their Dyson second-hand, and that usually means without the original instruction manual.

Your Dyson was designed to be used in a variety of innovative ways. It can be used in many ways around the home and in the car. Rather than me re-writing the Dyson DC07 instruction manual here, it is easier for me to direct you to an online resource where you can download a free PDF of the original manual for any Dyson vacuum cleaner: **www.tinyurl.com/dysonusermanuals** (all in lower case).

Your Dyson is fitted with two filters. There is a pre-motor filter and a post motor filter. As the name suggests, the pre-motor filter cleans the air before it passes through the motor.

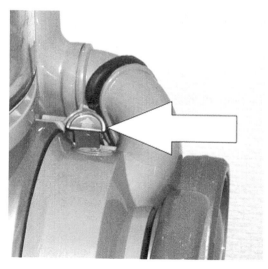

This filter is the washable one located at the bottom right hand side of your machine. There is a small coloured button, which must be depressed in order to remove the housing and gain access to the filter. The button is indicated in the photograph above.

Having removed the filter housing, the filter pulls out of the housing and splits into two parts for washing (it can be stiff if it has been neglected for some time, and may need a twist). It is a two-part filter. One part is a circular sponge with a hole in the middle; the other is the plastic carrier with a gauze insert. They look like this.

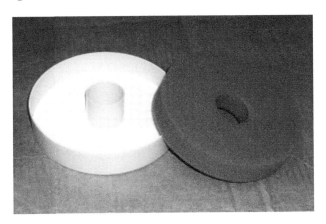

Dyson suggests only washing them in cold water and not using detergent of any kind. I disagree. I have been using warm water and detergent for many years without detriment. Many people put them in the washing machine too. Having washed both parts properly, place them in a warm place to dry for at least 24 hours or until completely dry. Occasionally, your old filter will be shrunken, damaged or too smelly to reuse.

You can buy a new after-market replacement for under £10 if you prefer to replace it. Many people buy a spare one simply to have a clean one handy.

A blocked pre-motor filter is the number one cause of poor performance in these machines. A blocked filter means less air passing through the machine, which in turn, means less suction.

If a pre-motor filter is badly blocked, it can also cause the motor to cut out after a short time. The motor is fitted with a thermal protection device that cuts the power if the motor gets hot. This is to prevent the motor from damage caused by overheating.

The other filter fitted to your machine is the post motor filter. As the name suggests, this is located after the motor to filter the expelled air. It is located under the circular grille that is below the cyclone unit. To access it, first remove the cyclone unit (as you would to empty the machine), and release the clips that hold the grille in place with a small screwdriver or suitable tool; many use a small butter knife.

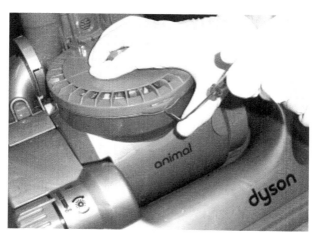

I tend to use a DC04 switch removal tool to remove the filter grille (see the resources chapter).

Depending on the age of the machine, the post motor filter grille will have either one or three clips to release it. You must release them very carefully or they will break. This can be fiddly.

Having released the grille, it lifts up from the front and then pulls forward to remove it. Under this grille is your post motor filter. There are two possible types fitted: one is a thin filter pad, the other is a HEPA filter. The two types are pictured below.

Basic machines come with a filter pad as standard. Better models come with a HEPA filter as standard. These filters are interchangeable without modification, so you can easily upgrade or downgrade your filtration by fitting the other type.

HEPA stands for "high efficiency particulate air" and filters must be manufactured to particular standards to legally use that term. They are claimed to be beneficial for asthma and allergy sufferers, because the HEPA filter traps the fine particles (such as pollen and dust mite faeces) which trigger allergy and asthma symptoms.

For the HEPA filter in your Dyson to be completely effective, none of the air should leak past it; all air should blow through it. The HEPA filter supplied with your Dyson when new had a rubber seal on the bottom to achieve this objective. Many HEPA filters supplied after-market do not have this sealing ring. It can be bought separately if you are particularly concerned about allergens in your atmosphere. Most people tend to refit HEPA filters without the additional seal.

A blocked HEPA filter prohibits air exiting from the motor as quickly as it should, making it prone to overheating. If you fit a new sealing ring with a new HEPA filter, you must pay extra attention to the condition of your HEPA filter in the future. Many people refit filter pads in place of HEPA filters. Filter pads are maintenance-free and are unlikely to block up, so the motor is less likely to overheat in the future.

Dyson claim the HEPA filter is a lifetime filter (lifetime of the machine is what they actually say). In reality, a HEPA filter will become blocked eventually, so "lifetime of the motor" might be a better description. For what they cost, why not simply change them once a year? This is likely to prolong the life of your motor.

If you are changing your motor, the HEPA filter will be contaminated with carbon, and occasionally damaged by the heat of the motor burning out. I recommend you change **both** filters routinely if doing a motor swap. If your machine has been used to vacuum up fine dust, especially plaster dust, it may be worth replacing it more often. You cannot wash a HEPA filter effectively (despite what some on the internet will tell you), so don't bother trying. A decent quality replacement is usually around £10 so it is quite an economical part to replace if in doubt.

Your Dyson does not like very fine dust in large quantities. In such an environment, your filters will become blocked very quickly. If you are using it to clean up after having had building work done (plaster dust in particular), or in any very dusty commercial application, or if you have hairy pets, regular attention to both filters is essential.

If a clutch (brush control) is fitted to your machine, there will be a knob on the side of the bottom housing, highlighted in the photograph on the next page.

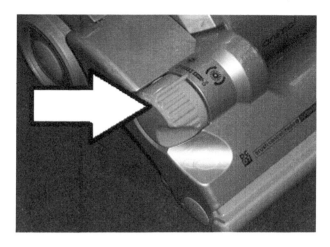

The clutched brush control system is the first identifier you should look for, as knowing if your machine is fitted with one will allow you to source many parts accurately.

The base models are all non-clutched machines (which are bereft of the afore-mentioned knob). On these, one drive belt runs between the motor spindle and the brush roll. On machines fitted with a clutch there are two belts. One goes from the motor spindle to the clutch, the other from the clutch to the brush roll. Machines fitted with a clutch mechanism were designed to seldom – if ever – snap the drive belts. This is because if the brush roll becomes trapped, the machine will give off a loud ratchet-like noise and the clutch disengages the drive (similar to depressing the clutch in a car). This gives you the option to stop the machine and remove the offending item without breaking the belts.

The machines with clutches fitted were sold as "all floors" or described as having "brush control". On newer Dyson models, they call it "multi-floor". By turning the clutch knob anti clockwise one click, you disengage the clutch, and the brush roll (often called a brush bar or a beater bar by some people) will not turn when the machine is reclined.

This ability to switch off the brush roll is to allow you to be able to clean hard, non-carpeted floors using suction only as opposed to combined suction and rotating brush roll action.

Models not fitted with a clutch such as the UK "Standard" and "Origin" models, were designed for homes with carpets only.

This remains a source of confusion for many people. They don't see why a machine without a clutch cannot be used to clean hard floors as well as carpets. I agree with them. It is true to say that when vacuuming a hard floor with a non-clutched machine, small pieces of debris can sometimes be ejected behind the machine by the action of the brush roll. This is about the only downside I have encountered. In my opinion, you will not notice or care whether your machine has a clutch or not; both will clean the floor well. Many people prefer non-clutched models – claiming they have better suction on carpet.

Machines fitted with a clutch will very seldom snap a drive belt. If they do, it is easier to source a clutch assembly (new or used) and replace the clutch as a single unit rather than dismantle a clutch to replace one or both belts.

For the determined amongst you, the clutch does come apart, and clutch belts are available online from a few suppliers. However, if a belt on a clutched machine does snap, it is often indicative of a fault in the clutch itself, making changing the clutch assembly at the first sign of trouble a better option.

Machines not fitted with a clutch will snap the drive belt occasionally. These are relatively simple to replace and this is covered in more detail in Chapter 3.

As you will no doubt have gathered, actual model variations, beyond colour, HEPA filters and clutches, were minimal. The basic machine remains pretty much the same across the range. The main difference is between clutched and non-clutched models. Any part from any colour of clutched machine will fit any other clutched machine. Any part from any non-clutched machine will fit any other non-clutched machine. Any parts that do not relate to the lower body which houses the clutch mechanism (or not – as the case may be), will fit any other DC07 machine.

All cyclones, wands, back hoses, bottom hoses, motors, chassis, u-bends, valve covers, etc., are all interchangeable across the whole range.

To get a general overview of how your Dyson DC07 comes apart, it is sometimes nice to look at an exploded drawing. Again, rather than produce one within the limited confines of a book page, if you want to see an exploded drawing that demonstrates how your Dyson DC07 is put together, I can direct you to an online source.

Point your browser at: **www.tinyurl.com/dc07schematic** (all in lower case). This will take you to a topic on the unofficial Dyson forums (that may not allow you to see the images without making a free account). It is worth making an account though. It costs you nothing and it is a useful site to discuss Dysons with others anyway.

Other basic maintenance comprises of easily removable parts that allow you to check for blockages. These are the u-bend, the valve cover, the cyclone and the back hose. The back hose is covered in Chapter 6, the cyclone is covered in Chapter 4 and the valve cover and u-bend are both covered in Chapter 2.

Chapter Two
General Troubleshooting

A principle of all Dyson DC07 machines is that they have a variety of re-movable parts, all identifiable by having different coloured buttons. If you see a button or a small component that is a different colour to the parts around it, it will generally do something. Usually, the coloured buttons denote buttons that can be depressed to remove something.

You need to know this, because Dyson DC07's have a number of access points with removable parts where you can check for blockages. Any blockage along the airflow system will affect the suction of the ma-chine, so you need to know where they all are.

The machine features a mechanism below the valve cover (re-moved by simultaneously depressing the two coloured buttons) that is operated by the machine being reclined or upright.

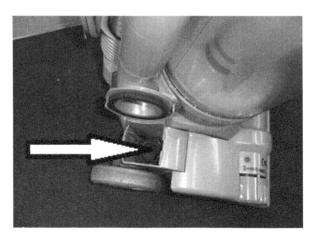

It is called the carriage assembly and is located where the arrow on the preceding photograph is pointing.

This diverts the suction to the cleaner head (the bit that sits on the floor where the brush roll is) when the machine is reclined to vacuum the floor. When upright, it diverts the suction around the u-bend and to the back hose and wand.

Occasionally, the carriage mechanism can become dislodged. This prevents the machine from standing up correctly. If your machine won't stand up correctly, it likely isn't picking up too well either. It may well be dropping some of the debris on the floor as well.

It was OK yesterday wasn't it? What happened? You were using it, and then it wouldn't stand up properly.

It's actually quite a simple thing to fix that anyone can do at home. You don't need any tools, you don't need any expertise. It is easier to show you how to do this than describe it, so point your web browser at this address: **www.tinyurl.com/dc07standup** (all in lower case).

That will take you to the independent UK Dyson Medic site where you can watch a short video on how to correct this problem.

If you understand the route of the airflow through the machine in advance, you will be better able to identify blockages and problems. Take a look at your DC07 and let me walk you through an arterial route map of the airflow.

Whether your machine is upright or reclined determines where the air enters the machine. When reclined, it enters at the cleaner head and continues through the small bottom hose to the carriage mechanism.

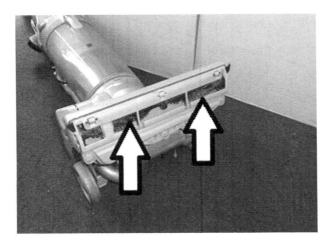

When upright, it enters at the top open end of the wand.

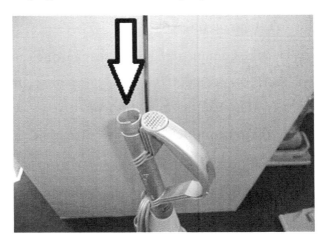

The carriage mechanism is where the moving air ends up from either opening.

From there we can trace the airflow through the carriage mechanism and upwards through a vertical chamber in the chassis of the machine.

It exits the chassis into the cyclone unit via the hole indicated in the left arrow on the next photograph, where the dirt is left behind by the clever trickery that is cyclonic separation.

If you are interested in the science of cyclonic separation, grab a copy of James Dyson's book entitled *Against The Odds*. In that book, he explains it quite well in layman's terms.

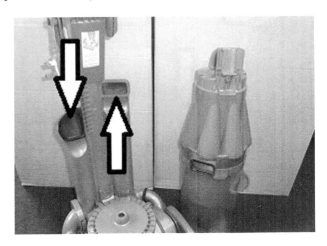

You can see in the photograph above the cyclone unit has two holes that correspond with the holes on the chassis when the cyclone is fitted to the machine. The D-shaped hole on the cyclone unit is air into the cyclone unit — the rectangular shaped hole on the cyclone unit is air out of the cyclone unit.

The air exits the cyclone unit back into the opposite side of the chassis, indicated by the right arrow above, vertically down the chamber towards the pre-motor filter.

The air then passes through the pre-motor filter and into the motor at the side of the machine.

It exits the motor above (below the cyclone unit) through the slatted grille, and is filtered again on the way out by the post motor filter. The route of the expelled air is illustrated in the photograph on the next page.

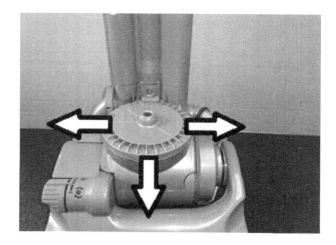

Now you understand the airflow, it is far easier to troubleshoot simple suction related problems.

Troubleshooting: Poor Suction

Many problems relate to poor performance or lack of suction, so we will start there. With a machine that has poor suction, perform these basic tests.

Check the pre-motor filter first (see Chapter 1 for details of how to wash and dry it). If clear:

Do you have suction from the top of the wand with the machine stood upright? If no, check the wand, back hose and u-bend for obstructions by following these steps:

- If you have no suction from the back hose and/or wand, you should eliminate a blockage in the wand from your investigation. When the machine is standing upright, there should be suction from the top of the wand. Slide back the coloured cover at the top of the wand to be sure. If you have no suction (or reduced suction) there, separate the wand from the back hose and see if you have suction at the end of the hose. If you have, then the blockage is in the wand tube. Now, you need something very long and thin to clear that.

• If you have no suction at the end of your back hose, remove it by pulling the clip on the opposite side of the lower mains cable retaining hook towards you, and it slides out upwards.

• Stretch it out and check for blockages. If the hose is badly blocked, a brush handle will do the job of clearing it nicely.

If you have good suction at the wand, but not from the main cleaner head:

Check that the brush roll is turning when the machine is reclined and running (the brush roll on clutched machines only turns when the machine is reclined in the "use" position). If not, investigate why not.

If unsure, try turning the clutch knob one click clockwise and test again. The brush roll on clutched models will only turn when the machine is reclined. On non-clutched models, the brush roll should turn all the time. If you have checked that the clutch is set to "auto", and the brush roll still will not turn when the machine is reclined, suspect a seized brush bar bearing or more likely a snapped belt or a faulty clutch. Clutches, belts and brush bars are covered in the next chapter.

If the clutch (if fitted) and belts are ok, but there is still no suction, try these steps one by one with the machine unplugged from the wall:

- Check that the brush roll is not clogged up with hair. If it is, see the next chapter.

- Check the bottom hose (between the brush roll housing in the cleaner head and the carriage assembly) for splits and blockages and ensure that it is secured properly at each end.

- On the left of the machine is a valve cover. The two coloured buttons at either side may be depressed together and the valve cover removed to check for blockages. Recline the machine with the cover out and look down both holes.

- At the back of the machine, at the bottom, below the back hose, is the u-bend. Remove it using the coloured clip and check for blockages.

- Remove the cyclone unit and the pre-motor filter and check both vertical chambers at either side of the chassis for blockages. Poke something down them to be sure.

By performing these simple tests, you are following the airflow from where it enters the machine right up to where it enters the motor. If you are unable to find any blockage on this route, you can check several other things.

Look at the pre-motor filter cover housing on the side of the machine (the one you remove to access the filter). On the outside, in the centre of the housing, is a small pressure relief valve (it opens if the machine is blocked to help prevent the motor from over-working). When the machine is running, check that it is not sucking air through there. If it is, it will be making a loud hissing noise from there.

You can check it in two ways. With the machine assembled, running and standing upright, slide the cover at the top of the wand back and put your hand over the hole where you might fit a tool. Within moments, you should hear the tone of the machine change as air is sucked through that relief valve. Move your hand, and it will revert to normal.

Take off the cyclone unit. Run the machine. On the right hand side of the chassis, is the rectangular entrance to the vertical chamber down to the pre-motor filter and the motor. (Make sure the filter housing is fitted during this test.) Put your hand over it. The suction should be **very** strong there. You should hear the pressure relief valve on the filter housing open almost immediately.

If you did all your other checks and are sure the machine is not blocked, but the relief valve is letting air through when it shouldn't, suspect some dirt in the valve holding it open allowing air to pass. There is a spring-loaded seal, which can be pushed back and forth from the outside with a blunt tool. Push it a few times; that often cures this. Some people use a small squirt of WD40 or a similar lubricant to help here if the relief valve is sticky.

It will strip down from inside if it is faulty, but it is easier to replace the filter housing if in doubt. Used ones are very cheap.

If you have checked everything else, and you are happy there is no visible blockage, you must suspect a clogged up cyclone. How to dismantle the cyclone is covered in Chapter 4.

Troubleshooting: The Dyson Does Not Run At All.

▶ **Caution: All work to electrical appliances should only be carried out by competent, qualified people in accordance with their local laws. Faulty electrical appliances can cause serious personal injury and death. Always take the relevant precautions, and if in doubt, consult an experienced engineer.** ◀

You plug your machine into the power socket and it is totally silent. The electrical circuit on these machines is quite basic and not terribly difficult to troubleshoot. You have only these components to think about:

- The fuse in the plug (UK models).
- The power cable.
- The switch.
- The internal wiring (switch to motor).
- The motor.

The fuse in the plug is unlikely to blow unless there is something else wrong with the machine. Nevertheless, check it anyway as the first step. Test it or change it. Assuming the machine gave you no symptoms to suggest the motor may be faulty and was working OK last time you used it, the power cable is your most likely suspect.

The cable fitted to these machines is a quite thin two-core flex. As these machines are now a few years old, many of these cables have developed internal damage that you can't always easily see.

First, with the machine unplugged from the wall, perform a visual check right down the cable looking for anywhere the outer sheathing may have split. If it has, twist the cable a bit and look at the wires inside. Your problem may be here.

The usual place to begin investigating next is where the cable enters the machine itself. This is the part of the cable that has been flexed the most, and thus the most likely to have suffered an internal break. The quick trick to test this is to switch the machine "on" (press the power switch a few times and you will determine which position is "on" – the lower position).

Plug it into the wall, and turn the power on. Grasp the cable near where it enters the machine and wiggle it about slowly in all directions. If you are lucky, the machine will momentarily fire into life with the cable in a certain position. This tells you that you have found the break in the cable and you need to either shorten the cable a few inches, or replace it to fix the problem.

If that yields no results, try the same "wiggle" technique where the cable enters the moulded plug. If the problem is at the plug, simply cut off the moulded plug and fit a standard plug. This is not a foolproof test, as the cable might not make a connection whilst being wiggled. Nevertheless, it can often save you a little time in diagnosis.

If your machine remains resolutely uncooperative at this stage, you need to remove the cable from the switch and test it for continuity on both internal (live and neutral) wires. If this is your problem, a new flex is the easiest answer. They are cheap enough to buy. You will learn how to remove it in a moment.

If your cable tests OK, it will be time to move on and check the switch. If you need to swap or test the cable or switch, you need to access the switch area.

Many people incorrectly assume the switch is at fault when a machine won't power up. In practice, it very seldom is the switch. However, it is your next thing to test after the power cable, because they do break sometimes.

As ever, unplug the machine from the wall first. The power cable runs straight to the switch. To access the switch area, look on the front of the machine, with the cyclone unit removed. Just below the power button is a centrally located T15 Torx screw. Remove this first. The front of the switch unit and the D-shaped power button cover come off together. To remove it, look at the back of the machine, behind the switch housing. The switch housing is further held in by two small lugs accessed from the back.

Get a flat blade screwdriver, locate the blade by the inner side of one of the retaining lugs at the angle shown on the photograph above.

Then give it a short, sharp shock away from you using the palm of your hand on the back of the screwdriver handle. Do the same on the other side. This will remove the switch cover unit. Remember (or photograph) exactly where the wires run for future reference.

Colours of wires can vary between different countries. In the UK, they are brown and blue. In the US, they may be black and white. Be familiar with the wiring colour codes in your country.

Having removed the switch cover, the photograph below shows you what it should look like now.

I am assuming you know how to test the two-prong power switch and flex using a tester (if you don't, you shouldn't be doing this anyway).

If the switch tests OK, and you have eliminated the cable from your investigation by testing it too, we are beginning to suspect the motor is at fault.

However, just before we do, check the cable ends that come up out of the machine chassis to the switch. Check them for loose plugs, splits and anything else out of the ordinary. You can also see this cable tucked behind the chassis, in front of where the back hose goes. Make sure it is still tucked in to its aperture and has not been pulled out or tampered with.

There is only this one two-core cable that runs between the switch and the motor. Because it never moves, it almost never breaks. The likelihood of the problem being on that cable, if you can't actually see the problem, is close to zero. The only thing that can occasionally happen is that one or both of the two plugs where that cable joins the motor can come away inside the motor housing.

At this stage, it doesn't matter so much if an internal motor connection has come adrift or the motor is shot. You are still stripping the whole machine down to check the motor now. You can read how to do this in Chapter 5.

Troubleshooting: Suspected Blown Motor

Often, if your motor has burned out, you will have had some warning signs beforehand. These can include an acrid plastic-type burning smell when it is running, the motor slowing down a little, running at variable speeds or a bubbling, popping noise. These are classic symptoms of a motor about to expire.

Usually what has happened is that the motor brushes have worn down and are burning as the motor turns, creating the symptoms above. At this point, many people have plans to replace the brushes and repair the unit this way. My advice is don't bother. The worn out brushes will have damaged the armature.

Replacing the brushes on the motor is seldom a long-term fix. Remember that the rest of the motor is just as old as the worn out brushes. Unless you are experienced in stripping motors down and reconditioning them, don't even try. Simply replace the motor with a new one. You can read how to do this in Chapter 5.

Troubleshooting: Noises from the Brush Roll Area

Noises from the brush roll area will only be one of several things. The clutch (if fitted), a problem with the brush roll itself, an obstruction, or drive belt related.

First job, with the machine disconnected from the power, is to remove the sole plate. Turn the machine so you can access the sole plate.

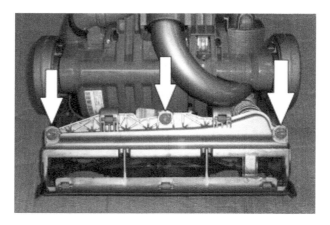

There are three plastic screws that hold it in place (Note: American models have a wider brush aperture than the UK model pictured above, but are otherwise the same). Use a two pence coin (or a maybe a quarter if you are American) to turn each one a quarter of a turn. Remove the sole plate so you can see the brush roll.

Turn it a little with your fingers. Does it spin quite freely? Is it clogged up with your wife's hair? If it is, use a razor blade or a Stanley knife down the length of the brush bar to cut the hair away and remove it.

Is the drive belt connected and tight? Check for obvious blockages and foreign bodies. If there is nothing visibly wrong, you will need to take out the brush roll and test it and the clutch (if fitted). Testing the brush roll, clutch removal, and everything to do with belts is covered in more detail in the next chapter.

I do advise you get a brush roll removal tool if you have a machine with a clutch. This will make the job of removing the brush roll and belt a whole lot easier. See the resources chapter for where to get one.

Chapter Three
The Brush Roll, Belt and Clutch

Here we are going to strip down the bottom of the machine comprising the brush roll, the belt/s and the clutch (if fitted). Parts and techniques differ slightly between clutched and non-clutched models so I will cover both separately.

The brush roll and brush roll housings of American-market versions of the DC07 differ slightly from the European versions. In the US, the market requires aggressive, deep cleaners, which visibly agitate the carpet pile and leave tracks. Customer feedback from UK users told Dyson that Europeans actually dislike carpet tracks, and are happy with the original UK specification machines.

US market machines also have much stiffer bristles on the brush roll and a slightly larger sole plate and pick-up slot allowing all the brush roll to be fully visible. The brush roll housing also differs in that it has a more protruding lip and is slightly larger.

There are two types of brush rolls: non-clutched machines have a cylindrical one; clutched machines have a twisted one. The two are not interchangeable. The belt runs in different places on machines with and without a clutch, so even changing the brush roll housing will not allow one type to be used with the other. The strip down procedure is the same for European and overseas variants though.

On the next page, you can see the two types of brush rolls used on UK market machines. The top one is the cylindrical non-clutched type, the bottom one is the twisted type fitted to machines with a clutch. Observe that the belts run at different points on the two types.

About Brush Rolls

You will learn on the following pages how to remove a brush roll according to which variant you have. Occasionally, brush rolls snap in half. In that case, the damage is obvious to see. However, in some cases, especially with non-clutched machines, brush rolls can be slightly bent. This causes them to make a loud noise when running.

To test for a bent brush roll: first, remove it. Hold it at both ends between the palms of your hand, hold it up near your eyes, and spin it with your thumb. If it is bent, you should be able to see that as it spins in your hands. If it is bent, replace it.

The other ailment they suffer from is seized or noisy bearings. That causes them to run noisily too. If the bearings seize, the brush roll may not turn at all or will turn with difficulty. This means the belt will slip, either on the brush roll or the clutch (if fitted). Often, a seized brush roll means replacing the clutch (if fitted) and belt/s too because the damage is already done.

You can twist off the end caps and check for debris between them and the roller bearings. Oiling stiff roller bearings is usually only a short term fix. If they are stiff, or seized, replacing the brush roll is the easiest solution. Some people replace bearings one-by-one as required. If you insist on doing this, Google part number 901768-03 or quote it to your Dyson parts supplier – they usually cost about £3 each. In my view, if one or both of the bearings are shot, just replace the whole brush roll for ease. They usually cost less than £15.

Many people believe the length of the bristles plays a big part in brush roll efficiency; they don't. Something else will wear out on your brush roll before the bristles wear down enough to cause a performance issue with your machine. A millimeter here or there on brush roll bristles won't make very much difference. The combined suction and the "beater bar" effect of the brush roll spinning is more important when dislodging dirt from the carpet. Don't get hung up about bristle length; as long as you have some, and they all look pretty similar, they will likely be fine.

Non-Clutched Machines.

First you need to remove the sole plate as described in the previous chapter by using a big screwdriver or preferably a coin on the three plastic screws. There are also three locating pegs at the front of the sole plate. Non-clutched sole plates are a slightly different shape to clutched ones. The two variants are pictured on the next page. The bottom one is the non-clutched one; the top one is the clutched one.

The sole plate on the non-clutched machine has the extra protrusion on it. That is a cover that shields the belt when the machine is running. It prevents any debris or even fingers getting close to the fast moving belt when the machine is running.

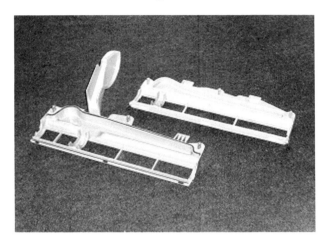

Having removed your sole plate, you need to remove the brush roll next. Now you have removed the sole plate, the brush roll is held in place only by slide-in locators in the brush roll housing and the tension of the belt itself. If your belt has snapped, the brush roll will simply come out in your hand easily.

If the belt is still attached on a non-clutched machine, and you haven't got a brush roll removal tool that fits this variant, look where it goes over the motor spindle. Insert a long screwdriver and manipulate it off the motor spindle. The brush roll will simply come out in your hand now with the belt loosely draped around it.

Everyone develops their own technique for refitting the brush roll and the belt. If your fingers are strong and dexterous, you may be able to do it with fingers alone. If not, some people use screwdrivers, thick string or large circlip pliers to pull the new belt through the slot (after fitting it on the motor spindle) in order to refit the belt. The photograph below depicts an engineer using large circlip pliers to refit the belt and brush roll.

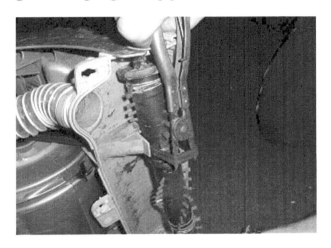

Opinion remains divided as to the best method of refitting the belt though. On these non-clutched models, some put it around the brush roll and feed it through the slot in the brush roll housing, slide the brush roll into place, and then try to stretch the belt over the motor spindle using a screwdriver. I don't like this method (especially not with a new tight belt) as it is too easy to damage the belt.

Others fit it on the motor spindle first and then use an old snapped belt or some thick string to hook around it and pull the belt through the slot in the bush roll housing and try to manipulate the brush roll under the belt and into position from there (I prefer this method).

After fitting a belt (or re-fitting a brush roll), be sure to observe the correct position for the brush roll ends and where the little pegs slot in before you release the belt again. Before you refit the sole plate, turn the brush roll a few times with your fingers to allow the belt to find its proper position on the convex profile it sits on and run true. This ensures you do not trap the belt when you refit the sole plate.

When refitting your sole plate, be sure you have located it using the three pegs at the very front into their slots before you put it into position to tighten the three screws. Refit it carefully, making sure you don't trap the belt as you do. Fasten it with the quarter turn on the three plastic screws with a coin. Make sure it all looks even and is a snug fit between it and the brush roll housing.

Clutched Machines.

Here I am going to detail how to remove and replace not only the brush roll but also the clutch as well. On a machine with a clutch, it is not possible simply to remove the belt on its own as it is with a non-clutched machine.

The sole plates of clutched machines are fitted with five little plastic rollers that help the machine travel on hard floors without scratching them. They can become broken or seized. You can get them from some online suppliers by quoting this part number for a set of five: 910427-01. But, they are not terribly cheap, and many people prefer just to obtain a replacement sole plate if theirs are seized, broken or missing.

The sole plate is removed by using a coin on the three plastic screws, and turning them all a quarter of a turn as described earlier. There are also three locating pegs at the front of the sole plate to be aware of.

If the belt is still attached on a clutched machine, and you haven't got a brush roll removal tool, pull the end of the brush roll from the housing at the opposite end to where the belt is.

The brush roll can be carefully removed by levering it out at the opposite end to where the belt is fitted.

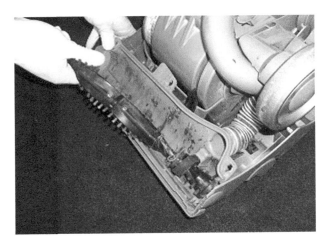

This will allow you to use the leverage of the brush roll to stretch the belt and better access the area around the belt to separate the two.

If not using a brush roll removal tool to do this, you will need either exceptionally strong fingers or a collection of tools and much trial and error to find the way that works for you; especially when it comes to refitting the belt.

Because the clutch-to-brush-roll belt on clutched machines is shorter than on non-clutched machines, it will be far easier to locate a brush roll removal tool to do the job.

A brush roll removal tool is always the easiest way of removing the brush roll and the belt on a clutched model. This comprises a metal bracket that fits onto your sole plate over the brush roll. The belt is pulled off the roll and onto two pins fixed to the bracket using a T-shaped bar with a ninety degree hook on the end.

A quick tutorial on using a brush bar removal tool (sometimes called a belt lifting tool) is in order here.

The photograph below shows you what one looks like. It is a two part tool as you can see.

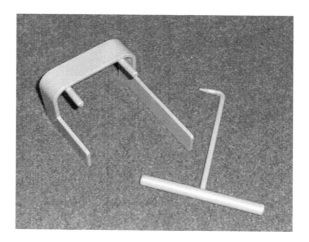

First, locate the metal frame over the housing with the arms facing towards the centre of the machine as indicated below.

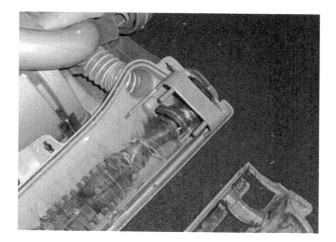

Take the T-shaped hook, and carefully place it under the belt using the pointed tip, then pull the belt up and locate it on one of the pins as shown on the opposite page. Take care not to snag the belt as they are quite easy to damage.

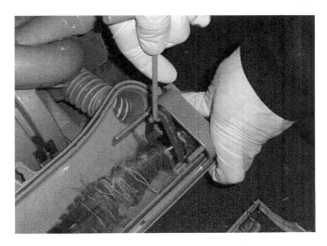

Now repeat, pulling the belt carefully onto the other peg as shown in the photograph below.

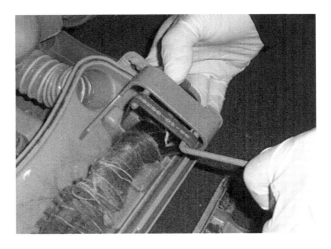

Having done this, the brush roll will easily come out. It takes a little wiggle.

To digress for a moment: you can see I have used a brush roll that is wrapped with hair and fibres and badly in need of cleaning here. I use a razor blade or a Stanley knife to cut off the hair and threads wrapped around them when cleaning them up during a routine service. It is far easier than trying to untangle them.

A brush roll that is caked with hair is a brush roll that is not terribly effective. Anyone with a longhaired woman or dog in the house should make cleaning the brush roll part of any routine service; clean it when you wash your filters.

To continue: the belt will now stay in place allowing you to easily clean your brush roll or insert your replacement.

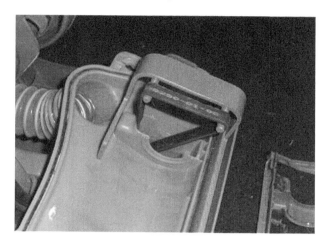

These belt removal tools are quite popular in the US, but for some reason are less popular in Europe. (Although, most belt removal tools will not fit non-clutched machines without modification.)

There is an importer of these in the UK though, whose details you can find in the resources chapter. Expect a brush roll removal tool to cost around £16 – £20 in Europe. It seems a lot if you will only use it once, but if you plan on repairing a few Dysons, it is an invaluable must-have tool, one that is usually only available to Dyson technicians.

Having removed the brush roll, disconnect the belt from your tool and move your tool out of the way.

You now need to remove the coloured clutch knob. I tend to use a DC04 switch removal tool (it has many uses) to do this. Insert the blade first under the knob and lever it off a little.

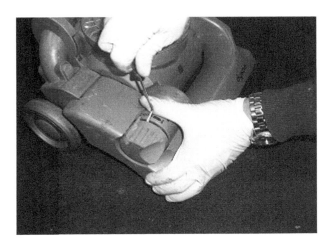

Then repeat this on the underside. The aim is to remove the knob by gentle prying top and bottom until it pops off. This can be a little tricky, and it is very easy to get frustrated and break the clutch knob while doing this. As with many things, it is quite hard to describe the exact technique. Once you have done it a few times you will have mastered it.

You cannot remove the clutch without first removing the clutch knob, so it is important that you develop a technique for popping off the clutch knob with ease. If you have access to any old machines, practice with them until you master the technique and know where the clips are.

You have now already removed the sole plate and the brush roll. That will have been much easier if you have a brush roll removal tool.

Next is the brush roll housing with the bottom hose attached. It pivots in the main body. If you grasp it at one side and pull it gently, whilst pivoting it slowly, one side will come out of the housing as demonstrated in the next photograph.

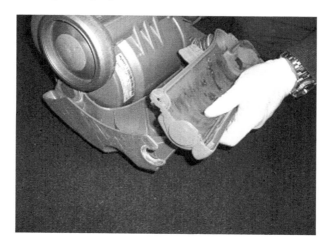

It separates easily only when it is in a certain position. This is why you need to pull it gently whilst pivoting it in the housing to determine where the release position is. Once you have done this once, you will remember for the future. Repeat on the other side.

When it is free at both sides, pull gently on the bottom hose at the far end. The bottom hose is twist-screwed onto the brush roll housing. It is screwed into a grey collar at the other end. That grey collar just slides on to the tube on the carriage mechanism it locates in with nothing more than a tight fit to keep it in place.

A gentle tug will remove the hose and the collar together, and the brush roll housing, with the hose still attached, will be released.

Now remove the inspection u-bend for ease of access to the screws (one cannot be accessed unless you do). Having done this, you can now see the clutch assembly in situ. The photograph on the next page shows how the machine should look with the brush roll housing, bottom hose and u-bend removed.

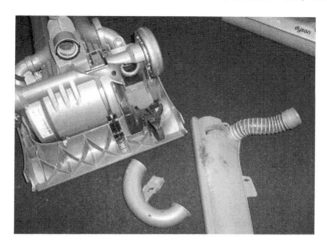

There is now the clutch cover to remove which is held in place with three Torx screws. You will need a long T15 Torx screwdriver to access the screws. I use one in an electric screwdriver, but a manual Torx T15 screwdriver is fine as long as the shaft is long enough to access the deeper ones. Find one with a 100mm blade or see the resources chapter for where to get one.

The first screw is recessed quite deeply and is here.

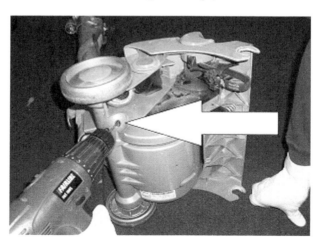

The second one is here.

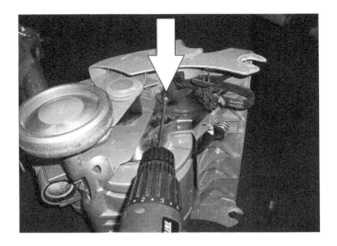

The third one is here.

Having removed the three screws, you are now ready to remove the cover. As it has likely been on for a few years, it can be stiff. You may need to wiggle it somewhat to release it. It sits in a very precise position and can be quite tight. With a little perseverance, and not too much swearing, it will soon come off.

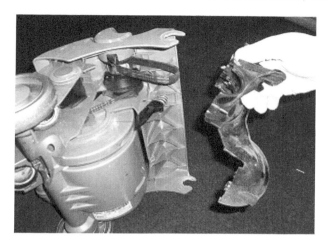

Now the clutch is accessible and can be removed. Remove the clutch to motor spindle belt from the motor shaft using a flat blade screwdriver. The clutch has no further fixings holding it in, but again, it is a tight fit. Grasp both belts and wiggle it and pull hard and the clutch will come out.

You are now able to fit your replacement clutch. Rebuilding the machine from this point is simply a reverse procedure to the strip down job you have just done.

Occasionally, there will be damage to the prongs on the main body caused by wear and tear over the years by the brush roll housing pivoting in it. Sometimes you may want to change the main body because it is scratched badly. At this stage is the perfect time to do it as you have done most of the hard work already. If you are changing your body or need to take it off for any reason, simply locate the plastic circlips either side as shown in the photograph below.

Remove them and the body will then gently pry apart at each side allowing it to be removed.

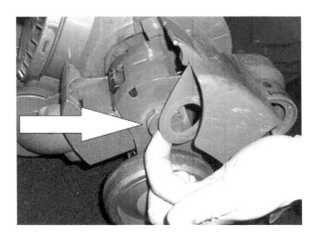

You can see how this is done in the previous photograph. Remove it with your fingers rather than tools so you don't damage it.

You can now remove the body away from the main unit, taking care to note that there is a locating lug that slides in a channel in the bottom of the motor housing.

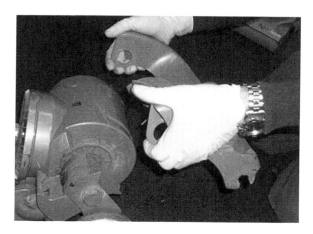

You may want to convert a non-clutched machine into a clutched machine or vice versa. This is easily done if you have obtained the replacement parts you will need. If you want to convert a non-clutched machine to a clutched machine (which is the usual conversion), here are the parts you will need.

- Main body housing (actually called a cleaner head).
- Clutch (with belts), clutch cover and coloured knob.
- Brush roll.
- Brush roll housing.
- Sole plate.

These are the only parts that differ between clutched and non-clutched machines. Assuming you can get replacement parts in compatible or similar colours, the conversion is merely a case of stripping the machine down as described in this chapter, and rebuilding it with the parts from a clutched machine.

About Clutches.

The clutch will occasionally need replacement. They do wear out. The telltale sign to look for is on the white roller wheel indicated below. Take a look at it. On a good clutch, the wheel will be mostly white like the photograph below.

When a clutch is damaged, or the belt is stretched, the belt will be slipping on that wheel and it will be worn, very black, partially melted or otherwise damaged.

You can replace the belts and even the wheel individually as touched upon earlier, but in such an instance, you will often find that other components within the clutch are worn too.

It can be a false economy to try to strip down a clutch to replace individual parts. Notwithstanding the fact that you will end up with clips and bearings everywhere that will prove difficult to reassemble, they are so cheap to replace that it hardly seems worth your trouble to even attempt to repair one.

Here is a photograph of a clutch that is too badly damaged to reuse.

You can see the wheel has started to melt with the heat generated by the slipping belt. This one is for the bin.

Do not be unduly concerned if your smaller wheel is not pure white. It isn't new any more; a little black streaking and a few marks are OK. It should have a smooth surface though. Flat spots, melted parts or heavy scoring render it useless.

To test a clutch, you must first understand the principle of how it works. It is similar to the clutch on a car: engaged creates drive; disengaged allows the motor to run with no drive transferred.

When engaged, both clutch wheels will be locked relative to each other. This means when one belt turns, the other does too. When disengaged, the wheels will turn independently of each other.

In order to test a clutch, first perform a visual check on the white smaller wheel. If OK, then grasp the belt that runs around the larger of the two wheels firmly so that wheel is locked. Then twist the clutch using the lever that protrudes in both positions and try to turn the other smaller white wheel using the other belt.

In one position, the wheels should be locked; in the other, the smaller white wheel should run free.

If you need a replacement, you can confidently buy a used clutch (ready to fit with both belts) from a trusted supplier. Around £7 – £10 will secure you a good, used one from a Dyson dismantler in the UK. They will test it before shipment so it should be fit for purpose and in good condition.

A new one typically costs upwards of £20, so a used one comes out at less than half the price and does the same job.

Chapter Four
The Cyclone Unit

The Dyson DC07 has the Root Cyclone technology, which consists of seven narrow chambers inside the main cyclone canister. Because they are narrow, well-used machines are prone to these narrow channels blocking up, and this reduces the efficiency of the machine.

There can be several reasons why you may need to strip the cyclone unit down. Internal cleaning and the replacement of broken parts are the main ones. It is good practice to strip and clean it when you fit a new motor. This is because very often, blockages in the cyclone create stress on the motor that can cause premature motor failure.

In my opinion, to service the machine properly involves dismantling the canister entirely and steam cleaning or pressure washing the narrow internal chambers. If you have a machine that performs badly after you have made all the checks described in the troubleshooting chapter, it is likely it is clogged up inside the cyclone. As mentioned earlier, your Dyson does not like plaster dust. It also doesn't like anything wet or damp, so if in doubt, its worth having an investigative foray into the cyclone unit.

The first job is to remove the cyclone top (the handle). **IMPORTANT:** When you do this, it is imperative that you pull the emptying trigger **first** and have the bottom circular waste emptying flap **open** while you do this. If you don't, the flap will remain locked closed and you will have no access to strip the cyclone down further without breaking something.

The handle is held in place by the three visible T15 Torx screws on the very top of the cyclone. Once these screws are removed, the handle is held in only by a rubber seal and dirt. To remove it only requires a little wiggling and pulling. It can be a tight fit, but it will pull out with some gentle persistence.

Be careful with it though, as the handles are very delicate and prone to break easily (this may be why you are taking it off anyway). For some reason, units that are blue or lavender seem particularly susceptible to breakage. Yellow, silver and green ones seem to be much stronger (there is no data other than anecdotal evidence to support this theory, but if your cyclone top is broken, I bet it is blue or lavender).

The handle will come out attached to the push rod that operates the bin flap like this.

There can sometimes be a small fin inside the cyclone on the shaft of the push rod; it slides off with persuasion (you can do away with it altogether if you want). Having removed your cyclone top, now remove the Perspex bin and the attached waste empting bin flap together, using the clip at the side of the Perspex bin. This is illustrated in the following photograph.

Now you are down to the bare cyclone unit. If cleaning it using a pressure washer or steam cleaner, it will strip down some more to make this easier for you.

The bottom of the cyclone can be dismantled a little further, but you will need strong hands and arms. The components are clipped together very tightly (they were not designed to be taken apart).

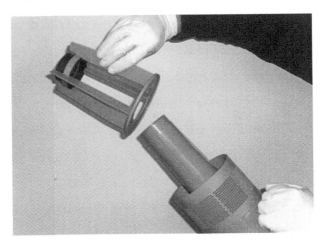

They can be released incrementally if need be by pulling hard at various points around them and listening for a small click as each clip becomes detached inside.

It is not essential to remove the last two bottom pieces of the cyclone unit detailed above for cleaning purposes. Most Dyson specialists do this because it speeds up the drying time after they have washed the unit. The unit can be washed with the bottom sections of the cyclone still attached.

The best method of cleaning the unit is with a pressure washer or a high-pressure steam cleaner. Brushing or spraying it first with a product like Traffic Film Remover (TFR) will help dislodge the years of grime. Clean every part of the unit from all angles. Pay particular attention the seven narrow chambers accessed from the top of the unit. Make sure you clear those of debris and they are totally clean. Look down each one to be sure; you should see a little chink of light if they are clean.

Clean also the inside of the cyclone handle and the Perspex bin with the bin flap attached. After washing the unit thoroughly, it needs to dry. You **MUST NOT** reassemble it while there is any possibility of water being left in there. Place it in a warm place. Shake it around. Turn it in all directions for a while. Make absolutely certain that when you come to reassemble it, there is no water left in there at all. I typically leave them at least 24 hours near or on a radiator.

I have seen some Dyson engineers with workbenches set up with hairdryers strategically placed to blow warm air through the cyclones to dry them faster and more effectively than leaving them standing might.

Did I mention that the cyclone must be absolutely dry before you reassemble it? *I think I did.* I cannot emphasise enough to you how important this is. Any water that is left in the cyclone unit when the machine is working again goes straight into the motor. Be warned!

When you reassemble your cyclone unit, it is basically a reverse procedure of disassembly. However, when you come to refit your cyclone top, take a look down the centre of the cyclone from the top.

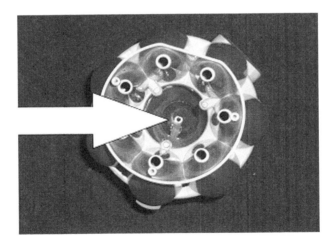

You will see a small hole at the very bottom. This is the hole that your push rod must be located into if it is to push the small spring-loaded latch that operates the waste emptying flap on the bottom of the bin. Observe that it is D-shaped, as is the push rod. The rod only goes back into it one way.

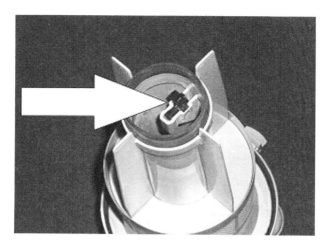

Be sure to test the rod is seated home correctly and that the trigger is operating the spring-loaded latch before you refit the bin and most especially before you close the bin flap.

The technique is to have your fingers in the bottom end of the cyclone, helping to locate the rod whilst simultaneously putting the cyclone handle back on. A little automotive silicon spray on the seal will help.

If the small spring-loaded latch pictured above is broken, it can be easily replaced by removing the old one carefully with the aid of circlip pliers. (These pliers have long springs loaded into the handle, and when you squeeze them, they open up, or spread apart instead of close.)

This part of the cyclone is very delicate, and extreme care must be taken not to damage the cyclone unit whilst removing and replacing the clip. If you damage the clip housing, you will need to replace the whole cyclone unit.

Do not insert the tips by the pivot point on the clip, that will break the cyclone. Instead, insert the tip of the pliers in exactly the point shown on the following picture.

You are going to expand the plastic just in front of the pivot point, and expand the plastic, by default, at the pivot point as you do so. Squeeze ever so slightly on the pliers, whilst pulling gently on the clip you want to remove and it comes out like this.

Some people like to dowse the area with a little boiling water before they do this in order that the plastic is more pliable. Fitting your new one is simply a reverse procedure of removal. Observe where the little spring sits before you remove it so you refit it in the correct place.

Dyson do not sell these small spring-loaded latches, or the bin flaps, or any other component you may wish to change in your cyclone unit. They prefer to sell you a complete unit (although some of those are already listed as obsolete).

However, if you contact a Dyson used parts dealer, you will get one for just a few pounds. Even if you are in the US or Australia, having one shipped from the UK (where used Dyson parts are abundant), should cost you only around $10 – $15 inclusive of shipping.

If you need to change a broken bin flap, there is no need to buy a bin assembly or a full cyclone unit. As with cyclone tops, blue and lavender bin flaps seem to be weaker, and they crack from the heat of the motor. Yellow, green and clear ones seem much better. They were modified slightly during production (they were made thicker – presumably to take care of the cracking problem), but the two variants are interchangeable.

You can fit any colour flap to your machine if you are unable to source one in the original colour. Different colours are all interchangeable. If you are having difficulty sourcing one of these bin flaps in Australia or the US, again, order a used one from the UK. They don't weigh a lot, so shipping is usually quite cheap.

Here is a little trick that will allow you to remove the old bin flap and install the new one with ease. Take the bin under your arm, with the hinge pointing downward, and squeeze it quite hard so it goes ever so slightly oval. This will open the locators just enough to remove the old flap and clip the new flap in.

There are two little cut-outs to enable this if you look closely at the canister. The next photograph details the technique.

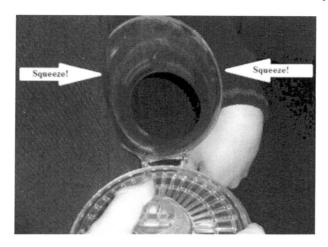

On some models, Dyson made clear flaps that will match any colour of machine. If you are not bothered about colour, and are buying used parts, as with cyclone tops, buy a yellow or a green one. For some reason, they seem to be stronger.

If you need to replace the bin flap push rod for any reason, it comes apart from inside the cyclone top with only one screw. The emptying trigger is attached to a small lever that forms part of a simple mechanism that is accessed by undoing the screw.

About Cyclone Tops

For some reason, Dyson refuse to supply the cyclone top on its own; even to the trade. They insist on selling a complete cyclone unit instead (where available). At the time of writing, nobody at all makes these after-market yet (although one is rumoured to be coming). So, nobody sells them new just yet.

This means unless you want to buy an entire cyclone unit, you need to buy a used one if you need to replace yours. Used parts dealers must dismantle an entire machine to salvage just one (and most salvage machines have a broken cyclone top just like yours has if you need to buy one). This explains why they are quite expensive to buy used. Especially lavender or blue ones; those are most in demand. Those in the US may have better luck sourcing one from a used Dyson parts dealer in the UK.

Often, you can buy a used generic all-silver one that will suit any machine. You may be able to get one in another colour that complements your machine if your colour is not available. I mentioned already that the blue and lavender ones seem to easily break. The yellow and green ones seem to be much stronger (pigments in the plastic some say). If you need to replace your cyclone top, and are not bothered about the colour, buy a yellow or a green one. It will likely last you longer.

Any colour DC07 cyclone top will fit on any other coloured cyclone unit. They are all the same fitting apart from the colour. Some later UK models and most US models have an extra "squeeze" locking mechanism on them to prevent the cyclone being accidentally removed while carrying the machine. This doesn't matter for our purposes. Any DC07 cyclone top can be fitted to any DC07 cyclone unit. They are all interchangeable.

Occasionally, you will only be able to source a used one that has the Z-shaped release button in a colour that does not complement your machine. You may want to change it for aesthetic purposes (or very occasionally to replace a broken one). An example being that many of the silver tops available come with yellow buttons (from Origin models) and you may want to change the yellow button for your blue or lavender one.

The coloured Z-shaped release button is designed in such a way that it does not allow for easy removal. To try to remove it will often crack the cyclone top itself. I remove them when I need to by carefully cutting a vertical slot down the back of the button I want to remove with an angle grinder fitted with a cutting disc. Care should be taken not to damage the cyclone top itself. You will probably damage the spring though.

In doing this, you are creating a slot that will allow what is essentially now two sections, to pry inward towards each other allowing you to release the securing lugs, and in so doing, the button itself.

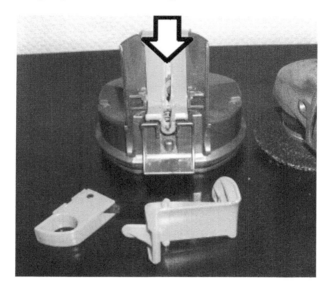

You can also, if you prefer, remove the button by using your large circlip pliers to gently pry apart the housing by the buttons. But, to do this, you will need a helper with a flat blade screwdriver to lever the button upwards out of its aperture whilst you are holding the housing open. That technique is not for the faint-hearted, and it is easy to break your valuable cyclone top this way. If you have a few scrap Dysons, practice on the old ones with cracked tops first. As with many things, there is a knack to this which you will only learn with trial and error.

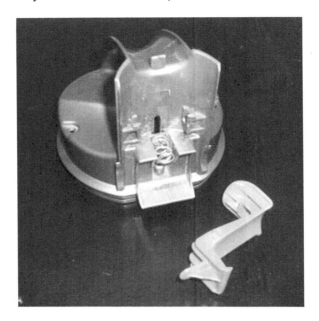

The picture on the previous page is what it should look like after you have cut the slot in the back of the button (the replacement button is in the foreground).

The picture above shows you the unit with the button removed and the new one waiting to be fitted.

To refit the new button, first make sure the spring is located on the cyclone handle itself on the little lug. Then the button slides into position from above. You will see the two little pegs on the button line up with two tapering channels. A firm push down, being sure the spring is behind the button, will allow the button to snap into its correct location. A smack with the ball of your hand might be a better description of the technique here. A quick, hard snap down is what is needed; not gentle pressure.

Removing the button from your old cyclone handle (to refit on your new one) easily will involve breaking the handle to do so. But that doesn't matter as you are replacing it anyway. But you may wish to practice the afore-mentioned technique with circlip pliers on your old broken one to be sure you get it right.

The coloured looped trigger release simply slides into place once you have removed the push rod, secured with one Torx screw as described earlier.

Beware of unscrupulous eBay sellers who are offering cyclone tops in the colours you want. As the desirable colours are in short supply used and currently unavailable new, some sellers are now spray-painting the (apparently) stronger yellow and green ones so they appear silver, blue or lavender. I wouldn't expect the finish on a spray-painted one to be particularly durable or the preparation to be adequate. I wouldn't expect them to be sprayed using proper plastic paint and lacquer either. As always with eBay, *Caveat Emptor!* Buy from trusted suppliers instead.

Many eBay sellers are selling used cyclone tops that have been glued and repaired also. These units are next to useless. A cyclone top that has been glued or repaired with fibreglass is no use to you. It will not last very long. See Chapter 8 for more on where to buy parts.

Chapter Five
Replacing the Motor

▶   Caution: All work to electrical appliances should only be carried out by competent, qualified people in accordance with their
local laws. Faulty electrical appliances can cause serious personal
injury and death. Always take the relevant precautions, and if in
doubt, consult an experienced engineer. ◀

I am going to assume you have read the rest of the book up to now. It will
do you no harm to read the rest of it beyond this chapter before you attempt a motor swap. This way, I can avoid too much repetition on the
subject of removing minor parts that you would otherwise know what and
where they are, and how to remove them by now.

Likely Symptoms of a Failed Dyson DC07 Motor:

- A noticeable smell of burning or a very strong acrid smell when
  the Dyson is running.

- The motor may sound noisy, laboured or be varying in speed
  when running.

- The motor may make a strange popping or bubbling type of noise.

- Smoke or sparks from motor housing area.

- There can be a high pitched noise from the motor, which may
  suggest that the motor bearings are worn out.

  Remember to make sure your Dyson DC07 is unplugged from the
mains before starting this job. It might be an idea to wash your pre-motor

filter now (unless you have a new one or a spare handy). It will take at least 24 hours to dry. Refer to Chapter 1 for instructions on this.

Replacing the motor is probably the most technical, and certainly the hardest repair to the Dyson DC07, and should only be undertaken by competent people who feel confident enough with electrical appliances to do it. This is not an amateur job and if you are not confident performing a motor swap to your Dyson DC07, please take it to a vacuum cleaner repair shop. Be observant of any local laws about working on electrical appliances also.

Assuming you are confident and competent enough, and it is legal to do so where you are, you will need some tools and parts. Here is what you will need:

- A new motor.
- Two replacement (or washed and dried) filters. Do not wash HEPA filters – replace those.
- Various flat blade screwdrivers (you probably have a selection of those anyway).
- A T15 Torx screwdriver with at least a 100mm shaft.
- A big cup of tea (or coffee if American), the wife and kids out of the house, and an hour or two to kill.
- A brush roll removal tool (if you want life easy and your machine has a clutch).
- A little washing up liquid (dish detergent in the US) or automotive spray silicone (the type you might clean your plastic trims with).
- Some automotive or household silicon or gasket sealant. Regular

Evo Stick glue will do in the absence of silicon.

Start by stripping as many of the parts that clip off your Dyson as you can. Take off the cyclone unit, the u-bend, the valve cover, the back hose and the wand. Next take out the pre-motor filter and the post-motor filter.

Now you are ready to get technical. **Double check the machine is unplugged from the wall first.** Remove the switch housing as described on pages 24 – 25. Unplug the switch and remove the mains lead. The cable that remains goes through a hole to the back of the chassis. From there, it needs gently pulling from the channel it sits in as the picture below shows.

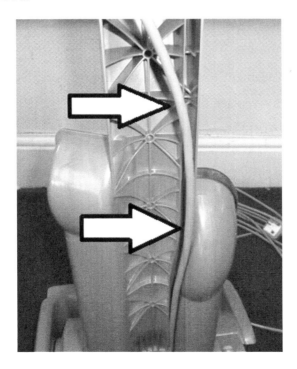

You can now see the cable where it goes into the motor housing near the bottom of the machine. Leave that as it is for now; you access the rest of the wiring a little later on.

Your next task is to strip the bottom of the machine down. Remove the sole plate, brush roll, brush roll housing and clutch cover (if a clutch is fitted to your machine). You will find how to do that in Chapter 3. It is not necessary to actually remove the clutch to do any of this unless it is faulty and you are replacing it at the same time. Take this opportunity to visually check the clutch and brush roll anyway.

You are now left with the chassis and the attached motor housing. To remove the motor housing and front motor cover from the chassis, there are four screws. They are the usual T15 Torx screws that you will find all over the machine. There are two where the white arrows on the photograph below indicate.

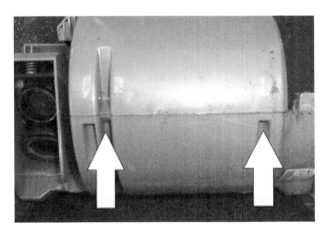

You will find two more that are in the deep holes in the chassis, and can be found where indicated in the photograph on the next page. Check the photographs carefully and be sure you are unscrewing the correct ones.

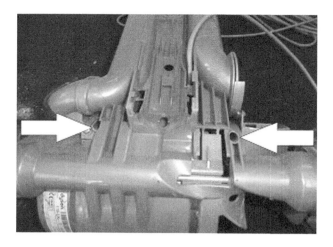

Having removed those four screws, the motor case can now be separated from the chassis like this.

The front motor cover can now be carefully removed. There is nothing holding it in place now. It just fits snugly against the motor housing. Be careful not to crack it as you remove it as shown in the next photograph.

Now the motor housing must be opened. This is done by removing the grey plastic retaining ring from the plastic housing. The two are held together by four plastic locating lugs that you can carefully release one by one with a screwdriver as shown below.

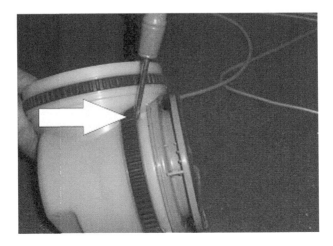

Now the motor retaining ring is removed and it should now look like the next photograph overleaf.

The motor comes out of the housing together with the black rubber that you can see. To remove it, I find it better to hold the housing in such a way that the motor spindle is facing the workbench, and pressing hard, putting pressure on the spindle and by doing so dislodging the motor. The motor will now come out as shown.

You are now able to unplug the two wires (observe which colour goes to which colour – they may differ). Next, remove the two motor rubbers, as you will need those to transfer over to your new motor. The top one has a little metal clip over it that can easily be removed with a screwdriver. The rubber then comes off like so.

The bottom one is held in only by the lip on the rubber, and comes off as depicted below.

Take your new motor and fit the bottom rubber. Then fit the top rubber and put back the little metal clip over the top rubber. Offer the motor towards the housing in order that you can reconnect the two wires using the spade connectors.

UK and European models of machine have brown and blue wires coming into the motor housing. Brown is live, blue is neutral. Most motors are supplied in the EU with black and red wires. Red is live, black is neutral. So, you fit the red to the brown and the black to the blue on UK and most European machines.

If you are in a country that uses different colour codes, such as the United States, familiarise yourself with the colour of the live (hot) wire that is in the power cord coming from the outlet. Make sure that you know which wire that is on your replacement motor in case the colour differs.

Many after-market motors supplied to the United States may not come with the black and white wires you might expect. As there are many manufacturers of after-market motors, I will not speculate here what colours they may be. I will simply caution you to be absolutely sure that you know which one connects to which one in your country. If in any doubt whatsoever, do consult a qualified electrician or the motor supplier.

Having correctly connected your wires, you need to get the motor back into the motor housing.

The next part is the trickiest part of this whole job. It can take some considerable time.

You can dust the inside of the casing **very lightly** with the automotive silicon spray here, or smear **a little** washing up liquid (dish detergent in the US) or other suitable non-flammable lubricant around it. Your job is to get the motor back into its correct position inside the housing without pulling the cables and disconnecting the wires inside.

The top motor rubber has a protrusion that must locate exactly through the hole in the top of the casing.

The problem is, apart from the propensity of the wires to become uncoupled out of your sight inside, is that the motor can move as it is travelling up the motor case. This means it is often out of line when it gets almost home, twisting it in situ is nigh on impossible, and you have to start over.

However, with a little perseverance, and perhaps some swearing, you will have the motor seated correctly back in the housing. But, before you refit the grey plastic motor retaining ring, here is a good tip: often, these rubbers when disturbed do not sit entirely flush with the retaining ring when refitted. This means after they are reassembled and run, they will make an annoying howling noise caused by air passing that seal (in the trade, we call it the Dyson foghorn). It only maybe happens with 1/10 motor jobs.

If you want to avoid unnecessarily stripping it down again to cure the "howl", smear a bit of automotive or household silicon sealer around the raised proud ring on the rubber before fitting the grey plastic retainer

71

ring (any automotive gasket seal type product or any product like regular *Evo Stick* will do – **not** superglue). Your intention is not so much to glue it; rather to ensure an airtight seal by creating a gasket.

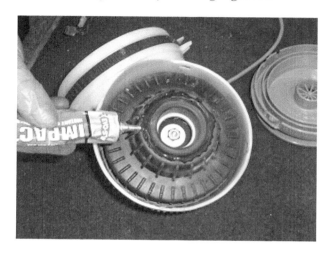

When I say a *smear*, I really do mean **a *smear*.** If you put too much on, it will ooze out and be sucked through the motor when you run it. You only need a smear. If you ever fitted a water pump on an old car, that much!

Now you can refit the grey plastic retaining ring. Observe that there is an arrow on the motor retaining ring (see the previous photograph). Be sure the arrow is pointing upwards when the housing is offered back towards the chassis. It simply snaps back into place.

There is a grommet around the power cable where it exits the motor housing. A gentle tug will seat it home correctly.

If the wires in the motor casing become uncoupled during the fitting of the motor back into the case, you won't know until you have the machine assembled again and it doesn't work. If you have the facility to bench test the motor in its housing before you continue, make sure it is clamped down well. It will jump violently when the power is switched on. I know people who got electrocuted by trying to bench test a motor this way. I recommend you wait until the machine is built up again before testing it. Stay safe and be cautious with electricity at all times.

You should now have an assembled motor casing with a cable dangling out in front of you. Next, refit the front motor cover taking care it isn't snagging anywhere.

Offer the cable back through the slot in the chassis it came from.

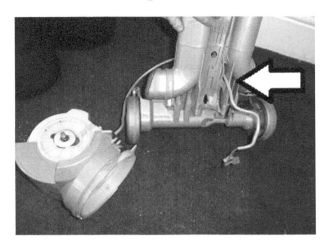

Slot the housing back into place back on the chassis, and put back the first two T15 Torx screws. Take care when doing this to make sure everything sits nice and snug where it should be. It is vital that everything is in place correctly in order that the screws line up with the holes for the rest of the reassembly. You may need to wiggle it around a little to be sure it is sat home snugly.

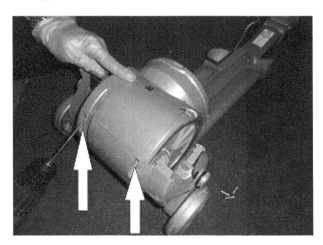

When you are happy it is all snug and in place, refit the other two recessed screws at the back to hold the motor housing in place on the chassis.

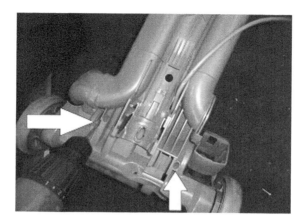

Now at the rear of the machine, start to clip the cable back into the long channel it came from.

A cloth over a large flat blade screwdriver may assist with this in order to not damage the flex.

When you get to the top, offer it back through into the switch housing area. The slot is on the opposite side to the long channel. Look at the top arrow in the previous photograph for the route.

You will see the cable passes from one side to the other at the rear of the machine. As you fit the wire home, be sure it is quite tight as you do so. Here it is pushed through the slot.

Then reconnect the switch and the mains cable (power cord in the US) observing how the wires are routed.

Take care here to ensure that you slot the cable protector back into the right position. If the cables are not routed correctly, they will foul the switch housing and it will not go back in place correctly.

It is the live wire that is switched. On UK machines this is the brown wire. That means brown into the switch, and brown out of the switch. Blue connects to blue.

Depress the power switch in the "on" position before refitting the switch cover and housing. The lower position of the pole in the "on" position allows the housing and button to locate home more easily.

When you have clipped the switch housing home, replace the single central screw in the front of the switch housing. That's the wiring done. You are on the home straight now!

The next job is to rebuild the bottom of the machine back up again. Start with refitting the main body.

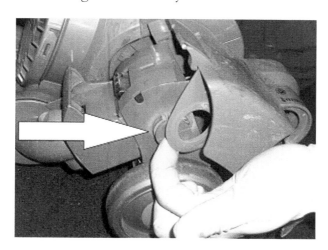

If you need a refresher on this, refer to Chapter 3. Don't forget the two coloured circular retaining clips that hold it in place.

Next, refit the bottom hose to its flange in the carriage mechanism. It just pushes on and should be a tight fit.

Next, the brush roll housing clips back into the main body. You can pivot it a little to aid you in this, but it should clip home quite easily.

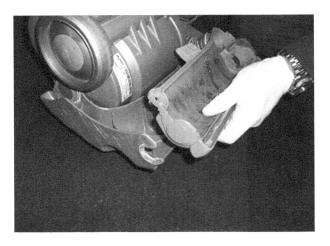

If your machine is a clutched one, refit your clutch cover with the three screws.

Next (on clutched machines), refit the belt from the clutch to the motor spindle. That can be a little fiddly, but a flat blade screwdriver and some patience is key. Take care not to damage the belt while you are doing this.

On non-clutched machines, fit the brush roll and belt together as detailed in Chapter 3.

On clutched machines, you can now refit the brush roll and the clutch-to-brush-roll belt. This will be much easier with your brush roll removal tool.

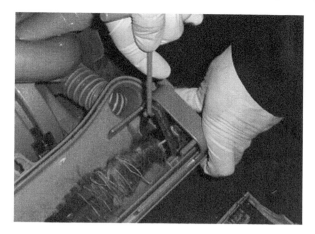

Be sure to clean your brush roll and check the bearings when refitting it as described in Chapter 3. Now you can refit your sole plate. Do make sure it is located properly using the three pegs at the front first, and it fits nice and snug with no unusual gaps anywhere around it. Secure it with the three screws using a coin. They only turn a quarter of a turn as previously described.

Finally, refit the simple clip-on stuff that you know how to do already:

- Cyclone unit.

- Back hose and wand.

- Bottom u-bend.

- Valve inspection cover.

- New post motor filter and cover.

- New (or washed) pre-motor filter and housing.

Now, plug it in the wall and test it. If you did everything right, the machine should now run beautifully. If it doesn't run at all, suspect you didn't line the switch cover up properly with the power switch (does the switch audibly "click" on and off?). Failing which, it is likely that the cables in the motor housing became unplugged as you slid the motor back into the housing. Whoops!

There is a video that provides a somewhat high speed overview of a motor swap that you can watch by pointing your browser to this address: **www.tinyurl.com/dc07motorswap** (all in lower case with no spaces).

Chapter Six
The Wand and Back Hose

Dyson will not sell the general public individual components from the wand. They prefer to sell you an entire wand. Several individual parts are available to the trade – but not all.

It is understandable though. As with the cyclone tops mentioned previously, if they sold certain small components to the public, their staff would spend all day fielding calls from confused customers who have no idea how to fit what they bought.

However, for the practically inclined amongst you (and if you have got to page 81, that must be you), rather than replacing an entire wand, anything and everything is available used for modest prices.

There isn't much to go wrong with the aluminum tube assuming the machine has not been abused. If you need to replace the aluminum tube, it is better to replace the wand itself as it is glued in rather tightly and you are more likely to break the wand trying to remove it. The other detachable parts are as follows:

- The coloured, perforated slide cover from the very top of the wand.
- The spring beneath that slide cover.
- The wand catch (that releases it from the body of the machine).
- The spring behind the wand catch.
- The swivelling cable retaining clip on the back of the wand.

- The glamour cap, spring, screw and washer from the cable retaining clip.

- The coloured insert in the rear tool holder.

- The curved trim on the very top of the handle (where the palm of your hand would be when using the machine).

I will detail how to remove those parts for you:

- **The slide cover from the top of the wand:** This part simply pulls off. First open it, and then pull it sharply (in the direction as if to close it over the wand tube). Instead of stopping at the "closed" position, it will pull straight out if you are enthusiastic enough with it. There is very little holding this clip in, but the technique required to remove it can trap the skin in your fingers if you are not careful.

- **The spring beneath the slide cover:** This part detaches very simply with your fingers once the slide cover is removed.

- **The wand release catch:** This part and the spring behind it are accessed by looking toward the bottom of it, and finding the two locating lugs at each side. Place a screwdriver behind either side, right by the lug, and pry off the lug gently. Then repeat for the other side. Be aware that the spring sits on little locators. To refit, just line up the spring, fit the top lip under the retaining ridge first, and then snap it back on the lugs with your hand.

- **The swivelling cable retaining clip:** There is a round colour contrasting cap within the clip, which covers the screw (they call it a glamour cap). Place a very fine blade down the edge of it and gently pry it out. You will then see the Torx screw. Remove the screw and the washer and spring with it (the grease is supposed to be there). The cable clip just comes off in your hand then.

- **The coloured insert in the rear tool holder:** If this is broken, your crevice tool will not stay held in the tool holder. Again, it can be pried out carefully with a screwdriver. The new one just clips back in place by inserting it at an angle, and then manipulating it back into place with a small snap.

- **The curved trim on the very top of the handle:** When you have removed the slide cover from the top of the wand, there is a Torx screw that you will see. Undo it and the handle top lifts up at the back, and then slides back to remove it (it can be stiff). The next picture shows you the position of the screw you must remove. I use two DC04 switch removal tools (they have a thousand uses) to gently pry the insert up and back out as pictured overleaf.

The handle insert then comes off like this.

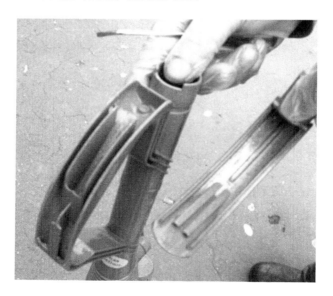

The Back Hose

The back hoses usually split near the top collar due to wear and tear. Most people tend to buy a new hose to replace a split one with.

The back hoses often get very dirty with prolonged use. Some people try to wash them. But, I am of the opinion that it is too labour-intensive to dry them properly due to the possibility of water lodging in the folds of the hose.

Stretching it out to dry and using a hairdryer down the tube is what some people do. I am of the opinion that a very dirty hose is a scrap hose, because the labour involved in cleaning it costs more than a new replacement. Furthermore, if you wash it, any residual water that is left behind is likely to get sucked towards the motor next time you use the machine. **Bang!**

To remove your hose, first remove the cyclone unit. From the front of the machine, look for the small hole near the base of the machine where the retaining clip can be just seen.

Press where the arrow on the photograph above indicates to release the clip, whilst simultaneously pulling the hose up at the back. It can also be done from the back by releasing the clip with your fingernail.

Then remove the hose as shown below.

Fitting a new hose is simple. It simply clicks in when you have located it in the two channels in the back of the machine.

Many after-market hoses are cheap and nasty (cheap eBay ones mostly). They can be problematical to fit and often pull out when the hose is stretched. Many cheap after-market ones also have a very poorly manufactured locking end collar that can be cumbersome to use.

The hoses supplied by the website we recommend in Chapter 8 are a few pounds cheaper than genuine Dyson ones, and I believe of a comparable quality to Dyson ones.

If you are determined to repair a hose that is split near the top collar (and I don't recommend you bother for what a new one costs), it can be shortened an inch or two. You need a very strong plastic and rubber glue. General purpose adhesive or superglue is seldom good enough. I use *Evo-Stick PVC Pipe Weld*. That seems to do the job nicely.

Take a look at the top collar on your back hose. Look at either side of it and you will see two small oval black plastic lugs. These need to be depressed simultaneously in order to remove the top of the collar.

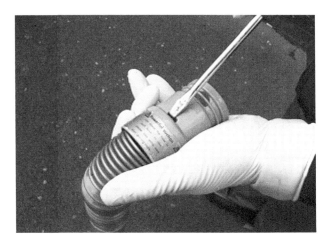

This is far easier said than done. Many people take the skin off their fingers attempting this. It is very easy to crack the grey collar while doing this too.

Having removed the collar, separate the black end cap from the end of the hose. Clean all the old glue off it, and trim the hose back beyond the damage. Apply the glue as shown to the black end cap.

The end cap can now be screwed back into the hose and the glue allowed to set. It should now look like the photograph overleaf.

Give the glue ample time to set, overnight preferably, and the top collar can be refitted by using the palm of your hand and some very firm pressure.

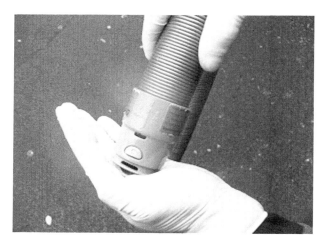

Take care to observe that the lugs relocate properly. Also take notice that there are two springs in the top collar that is part of the release button mechanism. Check that they are still there, and are working before refitting the collar.

As I mentioned already, I don't believe it is time-efficient trying to clean and repair old hoses when compared to less than £20 for a brand new one. But, it is something people often ask about, so I included it in the book for this reason.

Chapter Seven
The Chassis and Sundries

There are several reasons why you may need to perform a chassis swap. Dyson call it a "duct assembly" but I prefer the term chassis because it makes more sense.

A chassis typically breaks in several places. Where the wand clips in, there are four locating lugs. It is common to see one or even two missing. However, when the day comes when more than two break, you will be swapping the chassis because the wand will no longer clip home.

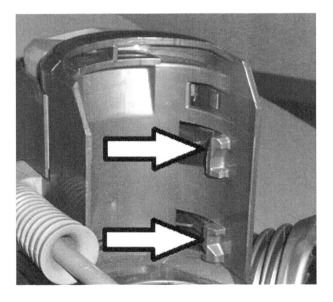

Another place prone to breakage is a little lug that stops the machine bending too far forward when it is stood up. It should look like the photograph opposite.

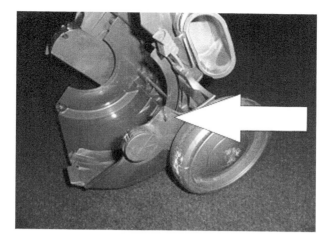

It often looks like this with a bit snapped off.

If you are perfectionist, or in the trade selling reconditioned machines, you will want to make sure this little lug is not broken. If you are not too bothered and only want the machine to clean the floor, do not be too concerned about it. Its only purpose is to stop the machine bending too far forward when it is stood upright. Think of it like a doorstop. If you treat your machine gently, it really will not matter if this is broken.

The area where the tools clip into the side of the chassis is another place that there can occasionally be a problem. If your tools will not click into the circular locators each side of the chassis, there are little parts you can replace if you can find them.

First, check that you are using the correct tools, and ones of good quality. Many after-market tools are of very inferior quality.

Some cheap after-market tools do not have the necessary groove in them that allows them to clip into the chassis correctly. Your stair, crevice and brush tools should have a groove around the collar as shown below.

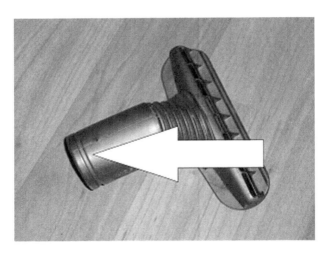

Some tools from the earlier DC04 and DC03 machines look almost identical to DC07 tools. Indeed, they will fit on to the end of your telescopic hose and onto the end of your wand. However, if they do not have that groove in them, they will not clip into the tool holders.

Many unscrupulous sellers on markets, eBay, Amazon and elsewhere try to pass off earlier specification tools as DC07 tools. Many manufacturers label tools suitable for the DC01, DC03, DC04 and DC07. However, if it does not have the groove, it is no good for your DC07.

If you are trying to insert the correct tool into the tool holder ap-erture on the chassis and it will not snap home, this is what to check. On the side of the chassis, by the tool holder aperture, you will see a circular piece of trim indicated in the photograph below.

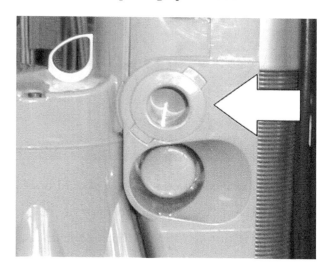

There is one of these on each side of the chassis. The far side of each of them, at the opposite side of the chassis, is the clip that holds the tool on the opposite side. Therefore, the tool slot on any given side is the other end of the corresponding clip on the other side.

Look down your circular tool slot (the one **below** the part high-lighted by the arrow above) and make sure you can see two clips that lo-cate into the afore-mentioned ridge on your tool. They can sometimes become misaligned, and tweaking them with a screwdriver can often align them again.

They can be removed and replaced if necessary. They come out with a securing clip on each side of them that a flat blade screwdriver will release. The next photograph shows you what the chassis looks like with them removed.

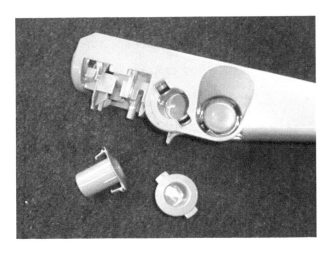

The wheels and axle is something that I should briefly cover. Over time, the wheels can become wobbly and occasionally fall off. The axle is a straight rod that passes through the bottom of the chassis. The wheels are slid over it, secured in place with a circlip on each side.

If your wheels are still on, but wobbly, you can pack them a little with small washers to firm them up. All you need to do is pop off the central cap on the wheel (Dyson call it a glamour cap) using a small blade, (A DC04 switch removal tool is ideal). You will then see the circlip that can also be popped off. Place a couple of appropriate sized washers on the inner side of the wheels as required. Then push the circlip back on, refit the glamour cap, and the wheels should be much firmer and now not be wobbling.

Chapter Eight
Where to Source Parts and Machines

Many people reading this book will either be traders of some description, or seeking to become one.

Those who are not traders will still want to source decent parts and machines at reasonable prices.

To understand the market place that exists, you should understand who is who, where they get their parts from, and what types of sellers to avoid.

Official Dyson Outlets

Official Dyson outlets, be it a local agent, auction site channel, supermarket, big store or a Dyson-approved website of some kind, will usually be tied to selling genuine Dyson parts and machines. This means they are likely not allowed to sell after-market, used or reconditioned parts. This means you will usually pay top price: full retail price. If you are reading this book, I think you are smarter than that.

Don't assume that genuine Dyson parts – which are often quite expensive – are inherently better than those made by other manufacturers. After-market manufacturers often address the design weaknesses that were overlooked when the original parts were made, in my opinion.

Many domestic appliance parts that must, for legal reasons, be labelled "after-market" are in fact OEM. OEM stands for "Original Equipment Manufacturer" which means they were made by the same company that makes them for the original manufacturer, but they don't have the original manufacturer's name stamped on them. This is quite common in the domestic appliance after-market.

You can find the same thing with automotive parts. You may buy a part from a Mercedes-Benz dealer that comes in a Mercedes-Benz box. That part may actually be made by a company like Bosch or Siemens instead. It could be bought using an alternative part number from an after-market supplier for less money. It will come in a different box but be the same item. Look out for "OEM" or "OE" descriptions when buying parts.

After-Market Parts

Seek out a reputable used and after-market parts supplier for most parts. After-market items – if of good quality – will be just fine if you seek well-made items and don't just buy on price point.

Other manufacturers only make parts if they are in demand enough that production runs, importation from the Far East, import duties and other fees make the item commercially viable.

For this reason, after-market items are usually limited to tools, back hoses, bottom hoses, filters, brush rolls and motors. The things people use the most.

There is a lot of cheap and nasty new stuff out there though. The cheapest stuff on the biggest shopping websites is often the cheapest stuff the supplier could get from China. Those people sell on price point only. Buy the cheapest you can find and you may well be disappointed with the quality.

Used Parts

Used parts (in the UK at least) are generally abundant – for now. Dysons have been manufactured for many years in great numbers. At the end of their useful life to one owner, a great number of them are passed on to dealers via waste disposal facilities and eventually end up with spare parts sellers to be dismantled. However, the UK government is trying to regulate the waste disposal industry (perhaps that should read over-regulate).

The European WEEE regulations, implemented in the UK in 2007, are responsible for this governmental interference in the waste disposal industry. This means that all items must have a paper trail from the waste disposal facility to ensure they are being disposed of legally. This paper trail, and all the associated licences and other associated EU nonsense is occasionally stifling supply to the used parts sellers. Certainly, it will eventually increase prices as costs will be passed on. It is a paradox that the UK government's attempts at making the country greener, is resulting in stifling the activities of those who are actually trying to recycle.

eBay

I have repaired so many Dysons for customers over the years that have been bought from eBay, that I cannot recommend it as a source of decent machines. It is a good source of broken and non-working machines in your local area though. Assume every machine is broken and a non-runner and you will not go far wrong. Assume every DC07 has a broken cyclone top – at the very least – and factor that into your bid, especially if you are seeking to make a profit.

There are also very many amateur people on eBay selling machines that masquerade as "reconditioned" or "refurbished by seller". Many of them are no such thing. Many are hastily cobbled together in order that they work acceptably for a very short period of time. The only people to trust when buying a reconditioned machine from eBay are those who have a glowing four digit feedback and who also have a real world business (bricks and mortar shop and/or proper website) specialising in Dysons. Those who are operating quietly from their garden shed are seldom a source of quality machines.

With parts – especially clutches, hoses, motors and cyclone tops – I have been so frequently disappointed with stuff bought from eBay, that I cannot recommend it as source of good used parts either. That is, unless the seller has a 1000+ and a high nineties percent feedback. Almost every cyclone top I have bought has been cracked, glued, sprayed or was otherwise faulty in some way.

The fees for using the eBay and Paypal consortium are so expensive for sellers (as high as 17% of gross in the UK), that it hardly makes sense for some sellers to send out a good item if they want to make a profit and compete with others. There are so many people nickel and diming each other on there and so many Paypal fraudsters enjoying free refunds for *items not received*, that used parts sellers are often not incentivised to send out quality items.

Added to which, many used parts sellers on eBay are those who also rebuild Dysons for sale locally in the small advertisement sections of their local paper, local websites, and markets or for car boot and yard sales.

This means they often sell on eBay the stuff they cannot or will not use themselves. In other words: their rubbish.

As for new parts on eBay, you should read the listings very carefully and not always go for the cheapest option. Again, only buy from sellers with four digit feedback and high nineties satisfaction ratings. Pay attention to their returns policies and who pays for that return. Disregard status levels like "Power Seller" and "Trusted Seller" – that simply denotes those who pay a lot of eBay seller fees, in my opinion.

However, with very high volume sellers whose feedback is in many thousands, this can often be used to disguise what is really a poor feedback record. The reason for this is that they receive feedback at such a rate that negative and neutral ones soon fall off the pages. A seller with a 10,000 feedback can have 100 unhappy customers on there and still show a 99% satisfaction score. If those 100 all say "this guy sells crap" how will you know unless you spend an hour trawling back through the pages?

Well, there is a way to find out that takes only moments. Go to the site **www.toolhaus.org** and there you can paste in an eBay user ID, tick the "over 1000 items" box and immediately get a list of that seller's bad and neutral feedback all on one page.

But, really, will you save enough on eBay to be bothered doing all this to avoid the likelihood of being ripped off? Only you know this.

I prefer to buy from sites run by people I can telephone if need be, and who exist in the real world. Not people I only know as *Joe456788T*. I can also possibly pay a little less for better items, because when people sell from their own sites, they are not paying the very expensive eBay and Paypal fees.

Local Websites

In your area, you likely have local free websites. Two of the big ones are **www.GumTree.com** and **www.CraigsList.com**. Between them, they cover most of the UK, Australia and the US.

These sites can be a good source of machines that you are able to buy and refurbish yourself (now you know how). As with eBay, the "reconditioned" machines are likely to be anything but (unless coming from a trusted seller with a verifiable reputation). However, faulty machines in your local area, you can often get very cheaply.

Many people do not seek to repair vacuum cleaners when they break. They just buy a new one and try to get a little money from someone for the old one.

Many people trawl these sites seeking machines to repair and make a little profit on. I have bought machines from such websites that were "cutting out and probably need a motor" for peanuts. When you and I know that the owner doesn't know they have a filter that needs washing, and that "cutting out" is a safety feature put there by design.

Where to Find Special Dyson Tools

Throughout the book, I refer to various tools that are indispensable. A T15 long shafted Torx screwdriver, brush roll removal tool and DC04 switch removal tool are the main ones I mention.

If you repair Dyson vacuum cleaners, you need to know where to get the special tools you will need to do so.

If you are going to repair many different types of Dyson vacuum cleaners, you can't do it easily without the special tools. Dyson won't sell you the tools. They won't even tell you which ones you need.

Apart from the standard tool box that everyone has, the correct special tools will allow you to perform virtually any job on any Dyson, from the DC01 right up to the latest models. If you are a Dyson enthusiast, a Dyson repairer, or work on many different Dyson models, you need the proper tools to do the job.

The belt and brush roll removal tool for the DC04, DC07 and DC14 is seldom available in the UK.

The DC04 special switch tool is not something you can get from your local hardware shop either. That is a trade-only tool sold through selected sellers only.

If you make your living repairing Dysons (or want to), or are a practical guy who mends a lot of Dysons, quit struggling without the proper tools to do the job! Observe the car mechanics that spend many thousands of pounds on Snap On tools. Why do they do that? Because every mechanic knows that having the proper tools to do the job speeds you up and increases your productivity. This means you make more money.

Don't be an amateur – get the proper tools to do the job. Point your browser here: **www.tinyurl.com/dysontoolkit** (all lower case and no spaces) and you will find the unofficial Dyson tool kit at the bottom of the page for around £30.

Where to Source Dyson Parts

This is my top recommendation for a good UK based supplier of Dyson spare parts to the UK, Canada, Australia, Europe and the US:

- **www.ManchesterVacs.com** – A superb source of new and used spare parts at reasonable prices. Usually slightly cheaper than Dyson UK for new parts. They will ship internationally and are usually cheaper than other sites and eBay on good quality after-market and recycled parts. Probably the biggest independent Dyson parts supplier in the north of England. They have a non-UK facing page that lists cyclone tops and a few small parts that you can find here: **www.tinyurl.com/dysonusa** (all in lower case – no spaces). But, at the time of writing, if you are not in the UK and it's not on that page, you should contact them with your order for a price delivered to your location.

Chapter Nine
Other Resources and Further reading

Nowadays, with the whole internet at our fingertips and Google to do the searching, life is much easier than it once was.

There are a great many supposed resource websites on Dysons, and Dyson parts suppliers out there. Many parts sites are "drop ship" sites that keep no physical stock and only exist in cyberspace. This means that when you make an order, they immediately order it from their suppliers who ship to you directly. At least, that's the idea. The problem with such sites is that if a part is out of stock or on backorder at their suppliers, you won't know until after you have paid. Some sites take many weeks to deliver items in this instance.

Unfortunately, not all of the Dyson-themed sites present accurate information. Many sites that masquerade as how-to sites and genuine information resources are fronts for affiliate sites (where your clicks to their other "recommended" sites earn them commission if you spend there) and others hoping to make a fast buck. Sites like this "recommend" items they make the most commission on, not items that may be the best buy for you.

Anyone can put up a website and say almost anything they want on it. Sorting the wheat from the chaff on the internet is always a hard task with a subject such as this. The sites that get high on Google are often the ones with the biggest advertising budgets, which does not necessarily equate to those with the most up-to-date or accurate content. Nor are they always the most trustworthy.

I have always found that internet forums are a most useful resource. An internet forum is a website for holding discussions and posting user-generated content. Internet forums are also known as message boards, discussion boards or bulletin boards. A sense of virtual community often develops around forums that have many regular users, creating a camaraderie one can enjoy. Forums are particularly useful for locating parts suppliers and picking up little tricks and tips. There is an excellent Dyson forum in the sites below.

There are two unofficial Dyson related sites I have found to be useful, that I feel able to recommend here:

- **www.DysonMedic.co.uk** – A Dyson-themed blog site that is a mine of information.

- **www.DysonForums.com** – A portal to a friendly discussion forum where one can discuss everything to do with Dysons with fellow enthusiasts. It costs nothing to join, you won't get spammed by them, and it is a great place to ask further advice if you have a problem with your Dyson. If you are a Dyson enthusiast, it's also a great place to give advice and share your knowledge with others.

Using the sites above, you will be able get any further practical advice you may need.

There are, of course, many sites across the world that offer Dyson advice. Personally, I have found sites like *Yahoo Answers* and *Fixya* to be often full of incorrect information. I prefer sites where you can get to the information you need pretty quickly and find it is usually correct.

Dyson has several websites around the world. Their website is designed in such a way that if you visit **www.dyson.com** it will direct you to your own country's site without asking you. However, if you are nosey, and know how to use a free public internet proxy, and are so inclined, you can bypass that and navigate directly to the foreign market sites. The official Dyson sites always make for interesting reading for any Dyson enthusiast. It's usually the first place you can find information on new Dyson products.

I hope you enjoyed this book and I hope you will use the information to keep many more Dyson vacuum cleaners working hard and out of the landfill sites.

I have been given a dedicated topic on the unofficial Dyson discussion forums where you are welcome to give me feedback on this book. You can also tell me about any errors or omissions that you feel should be corrected or included in the next edition. You can even drop by just to say hello! Go straight to the topic by pointing your browser here: **www.tinyurl.com/tellangus** (all in lower case).

If you bought this book from Amazon, eBay, Asda/Wal-Mart, Tesco or a similar internet site, I would very much appreciate feedback or a review from you on that site if you have a few moments to spare. Your feedback is important and tells me if you enjoyed the book, found it useful, and if my hard work putting it all together was worth it.

Keep on vacuuming!